For my beautiful Tiny grandma, the center of us.
No day has been as bright.

Tiny

and The Boy Who Loved Her

Written and Illustrated by Tracy Marie

There once was a tiny Grandma and a three-year-old boy who loved her.

His name was Hayden, and everyone
called her Tiny.

Hayden would go to her house to visit almost every day. Tiny was always in the mood to play with cars, tell stories, or play card games with him.

Even though he didn't understand how to play, she would always let him turn the cards over and that was fun enough for him.

At lunchtime, Tiny always shared her food with Hayden.

It made her smile to be able to eat it together, but then again, she was always happiest anytime he was near.

Every holiday was spent with his Tiny, Easter was her favorite of them all. She always got her own basket and shared the candy with Hayden.

On Christmas, her favorite part was watching everyone else open their gifts and seeing their smiles.

The 4th of July was also fun; the beautiful fireworks always amazed her.

One day, Hayden got to Tiny's house only to find that Tiny wasn't feeling well. He stayed by her bedside but all she did was sleep...

The next day, even with the new medicine she was given, she still could not get out of bed. Everyone around Hayden and Tiny seemed very sad and many of them started to say goodbye but he couldn't understand why. *'She isn't leaving,'* he thought, *'maybe they were.'*

A couple of days passed and Hayden didn't get to go and see Tiny. Hayden's parents seemed very sad, and he even saw his mom cry. Finally, the time came to go to Tiny's house, and Hayden was very excited, but when he got there, Tiny wasn't in her bed. The room looked the same but she wasn't anywhere to be found.

Hayden was very sad. He took his favorite picture of Tiny to his Dad and asked him where she was. Dad explained to him that Tiny was gone, and that he wouldn't be able to see her again. When Hayden asked where she had gone, Dad said that she was in a special place high in the clouds and that she was okay there.

Hayden thought about what his Dad had said for a very long time until finally, he had a great idea. *'I'll look for her!'* he thought. His binoculars could surely see that far but all he could see was clouds.

Everywhere Hayden went, he searched for her. As time passed, Hayden also started to come up with new ideas on how he would be able to see and rescue her from the clouds. He remembered that she was the happiest when she was with him, and that he was happiest when he was with her.

His first idea was to take a rocket! A rocket could definitely go high enough to reach her on any cloud.

Hayden asked his dad to help him call a rocket
ship guy to rent a rocket but it didn't happen.

Hayden had another idea—a helicopter! *'That would be a fun and safe way to get her,'* he thought.

An even better idea was a plane! He could parachute down to her. *'She would love that,'* he thought to himself, but how would they get back down?

Maybe, in a hot air balloon. *'That's perfect!'* he thought. Tiny could get in the basket with him, and they could float away together, but, what if it's to windy? That could be scary.

How about a Ferris wheel? Hayden went to an amusement park once, and he remembered how high up into the sky it went. *'That has to be close enough to the clouds,'* he thought.

Idea after idea popped into Hayden's head
until one day, he realized that he couldn't
really do any of those things. He missed her so
much, and his heart was broken.

That night, after Hayden went to sleep
he had a dream.

He was on a cloud, and on that cloud, with him, was Tiny! They talked and shared a snack as they had always done before. Both of them were happy and together again.

They stayed that way for awhile until Hayden started to cry. He told her how he had tried to look everywhere for her but she wasn't anywhere to be found. He told her how much he missed her, and how his heart hurt every day.

Tiny told him that she missed him too and explained to him that even though it would be different now, she would always be with him. "How?" he asked her. Tiny pointed to his heart and said, "I'll always be right there because I love you and you love me.

We can meet in your dreams when you go to sleep. We can go places and do things anytime, anywhere. Even things I was to tired to do before!"

So from that night on, they did exactly that. Hayden dreamed of fun things to do with Tiny. They took plane rides.

They even got to take a trip in a hot air balloon! (Only on a day when the wind wasn't scary of course.)

They went to an amusement park and got to ride on every single ride — even the Ferris wheel.

Hayden met Tiny in his dreams night after night, and as the time passed, it was time for him to start school. Even though he was scared, he knew deep down that he could look into his heart and Tiny would be there to help him through it.

Things will never be like they were before but no matter what, he and Tiny could always be together and happy in his dreams and his heart.